salmonpoetry40

Publishing Irish & International Poetry Since 1981

the arts council
an chomhairle ealaíon

funding
literature
artscouncil.ie

Twenty-six Letters of a New Alphabet

Anne Tannam

Published in 2021 by
Salmon Poetry
Cliffs of Moher, County Clare, Ireland
Website: www.salmonpoetry.com
Email: info@salmonpoetry.com

ISBN 978-1-912561-31-5

Cover & Section Images: *Claire Murphy*
Cover Design & Typesetting: *Siobhán Hutson*

Printed in Ireland by Sprint Print

Salmon Poetry gratefully acknowledges the support of
The Arts Council / An Chomhairle Ealaíon

For Neil,

who keeps *my suspect edifice upright in air, as Atlas did the sky*

Acknowledgements

Thanks to the editors of the following publications, programmes or websites in which some of the poems, or versions of the poems, first appeared:

Autonomy (Binary Press), *Banshee Lit, Between Two Worlds* (Yoda Press), *The Blue Nib, Burning Bush 2, Crannóg Magazine, Drawn to the Light Press, Empty House Anthology* (Doire Press), *Enthralled, Flare, The Music Of What Happens* (New Island Press) *The North, Orbis, Reading the Future* (Hodges Figgis), *RTÉ Lyric FM, Skylight47, Poetry Ireland Review, The Pickled Body,* and *Two Meter Review.*

Thank you to Jessie and Siobhán at Salmon Poetry for doing what they do with such warmth and grace. A huge debt is owed to Fióna Bolger, Alvy Carragher, Frank Jordan, Eithne Lannon and Claire Murphy for their insightful and encouraging feedback on various drafts of this collection. Thanks to Claire Murphy for the artwork for the cover. Thanks also to Amanda Bell for her copy-editing. Thank you to Mary O'Donnell, Liz McSkeane and Maurice Devitt for their very kind words about the collection. A very special thanks to all the gang at Dublin Writers' Forum who were often the first new eyes to see many of these poems. Thanks to Diego Garrido for creating my new poetry website. Thanks to my three brothers: David, Donal and Gerard, for their support and companionship over the last eight years as we navigated the illness and the death of our parents. As always and forever, love and thanks to my family (cue the opening strains of *The Wind Beneath My Wings*): Neil, Claire, Aislinn, Sian and Darragh.

Contents

Once for each thing. Just once;
no more. And we too,
just once. And never again.
But to have been
this once, completely, even if only once:
to have been at one with the earth,
seems beyond undoing.

— Rainer Maria Rilke, *Duino Elegies*

Turning fifty-two (i)

It's taken until now
to tune into the
miraculous presence of birds.

I knew there were birds before—
I'd heard them singing.

Not like this—
not like the earth depended on it.

Morning Pages

I write the blue of the sky, the beads of condensation
on the skylight, the chill coming up the attic stairs,
the sound of my fingers on the keyboard.
I write the brown leather of my mother's purse on the desk,
her fifteen-year-old eyes looking at me from the black
and white photo on the wall. I write the ache.

I write the heat coming from the radiator beside me,
the coarse feel of the woollen throw across my knees,
the house creaking around me, the knowledge of Neil's
steady breathing. I write the comfort.
I write the frame of Aislinn's door, the remnants
of Claire's artwork, Darragh stirring downstairs.
I write the day the house is empty of children.
I write the relief. I write the grief.

I write the colour of the sky on my run this morning,
birdsong, the flutter of bags, shredded and ragged,
caught in the branches of trees, the leaves budding into bloom.
I write the heron flying over houses, swans by the canal nesting,
the thrumming energy of spring. I write the cracks on the footpath,
the uneven concrete, Sian appearing on the road in front of me.
I write the joy.

I write my mind's eye remembering a beach,
my eight-year-old self turning cartwheels across the sand,
my fifty-two-year old body in awe of her.
I write the flow of the river beneath the river, the sound of water
rushing over stones, the brown hush of the riverbed.

I write my ninety-seven-year-old father, the veins on his hands,
his bony knuckles, the fragile length of him, the stubborn length of him.
I write my mother's death. I write the stillness of her body.
I write the dream of my own dying, the dream of my own death.

I write the pigeons cooing on the roof. I write the day beckoning.

Opposite and Equal Reaction

When you have a home
the morning beckons.

How does it feel to stand in your attic,
the house quiet and sleeping around you,
the open skylight an invitation
to fill your lungs with sweet clean air;
breathe and breathe until buoyant,
float easily out the window and up,
up over the trees and houses
into the colours of the early morning sky?

When you lose your home
you lose the morning light.

How does it feel to stand on the street,
your house erased beneath rubble,
nothing between you and cold concrete,
nothing but dirty water churning underfoot,
the night air filling your raw lungs,
a pinprick of darkness spreading,
spreading, the sky doubled over,
gasping for breath?

Home Sweet Home

i

Little pig, little pig, let me come in.
No, no, not by the hair on my chinny chin chin.
Then I'll huff, and I'll puff, and I'll blow your house in.

ii

At night when IKEA shoppers leave,
their trolleys piled high with picture frames,
picnic essentials for al fresco dining, cushions,
bedding, scented candles, bathroom accessories,

a trolley is dragged backwards up the escalator,
reversing along the designated pathway,
a hand returning, item after item to their places,
slowly emptying the trolley of its contents.

iii

We avoid passing our house on our way to school,
though it means an extra twenty minutes walking;
on wet days the kids get drenched and there's
nowhere to hang wet clothes in the B&B.

iv

Jack has the dream again: he's standing in the lane behind their old house,
face pressed against the garden door. There's Darren from his old school
splashing in the paddling pool that Ma threw out years ago,
splashing and laughing like it's his back garden, his toys on the grass,
his treehouse, and Jack shouts at him, *Leave my fucking toys alone*,
but Darren doesn't turn round, can't hear Jack's muffled words screamed
into the pillow.

v

Have you no home to go to?

vi

And I am praying to God on high,
And I am praying Him night and day,
For a little house—a house of my own,
Out of the wind's and the rain's way.

Intrusion

I can't tell you about India
but I can speak with some authority
about how that first morning,
out my fifth-floor window
overlooking a piece of wasteland
beside a small lake, I saw a man
squat down as if in the privacy
of his own bathroom, and I can tell you
with absolute authority
of the flicker of shame l felt, as if
I had walked in on him
without first knocking.

Don't Look Back

The haversack smells of aniseed
and lemons. She breathes deeply,
eyes closed, shutting out the sound
of their village uprooting.
He moves from room to room,
memorizing each length and breadth,
locking doors behind him.

She takes the stairs two steps at a time,
child held tightly in her arms.
After the border, where will we go?
His mouth searches for an answer,
eyes running for cover
as the front door opens,
emptying them out
onto unfamiliar streets.

Covering Ground

i

Once, I measured the distance I'd travelled in footsteps:
one foot, then the other, uninterrupted.

Can you measure the distance you've travelled?
Does the house that raised you still exist?

I only ask because I seek to understand distance.
Forgive my questions if they cause you pain.

ii

Water will not hold the imprint of a foot.
            Sand will temporarily hold the imprint of a foot.
                    Sand will also hold the imprint of a body,
                            however small the body,
                                    but only temporarily.

iii

Google Maps can measure certain distances;
                    It understands kilometres.
It understands certain delays which may lead
                    to interruptions to your journey.
It does not understand hesitation.

iv

Before measuring begins, the following information must be provided:
- the size of one's foot
- the time of one's last meal
- the location of any injuries
- the weight across one's shoulders.

v

Adverse conditions

are known

to cause

severe in terr up tions

to one's

journey time.

vi

Shoes can be replaced, if you can afford to replace them,
or if someone gives you a replacement pair of shoes.
Your feet cannot be replaced, even if the originals
are worn down to the bone.

vii

Did you arrive in one piece?
That is to say did all the pieces of you travel the distance?

I only ask because I seek to understand distance.
Forgive my questions if they cause you pain.

A thousand and one days later

he arrives
sets up camp
in a borrowed room
lays his young old head
upon the pillow
and sleeps

dreams three years
have not passed
in a blur of movement
dreams he's sixteen again
the sky above his city
clenching unclenching
ruthlessly erasing
all traces of home

wakes to the impossible
silence of a quiet sky
takes in the dimensions
of the borrowed room
unclenches his mind
imagines in one corner

a small Christmas tree
its soft pinpricks of
coloured light

beaconing

hearth

home

his

The Safety of Home

During a Hindu festival
in traffic-jammed Chennai,
the evening an oven of noise
smell and colour, crowds push in
around us, almost separating me
from our group; I feel Vatsala
slip her hand into mine—
and it is my mother's hand,
she is my mother's love.

Finds her way

by shadowing trees

follows feet-first
the scent of inland water

knows she's home
when underfoot
the earth hums
green in the key of O

Tethered to these Times and Places

On the stretch of canal that runs
between Golden Bridge and Blackhorse Inn,
swans absorb the early morning light.

The garage door opens
and in he comes, bringing with him
the smell of rain, the curve of the sky.

Between pedestrian lights and the turn
for home, I see my mother up ahead,
pulling her tartan trolley.

Light from the landing catches
a mess of books and toys, settles on
small bodies sleeping.

At Islandbridge, the river imagines
a child, blond head bobbing,
endless sunlight dancing around him.

The Pigeon House, roosting in the arms
of Dublin Bay, the lighthouse beckoning
us out to sea.

A Reasonable Request

She's free to go anywhere
she desires in the castle—
except one little room.

One small room off-limits.
That's not much to ask.

One little room.
Everywhere else she is free to go.
Everything else is hers to enjoy:

endless rooms to decorate as she pleases,
beautiful gardens to explore with friends.

See how much he is willing to give her.
See how far he is willing to go.

One little room.
Not too much to ask.

Never mind his terrible beard.
Never mind the rest of the story.

Role Models

Referring to it as *the job*,
Dad first, then my eldest brother,
would leave the house,
head out to bandit country
where *the lads at work*—
a self-sufficient tribe of rebels—
ruled their world from 8 to 5,
far from the reach of bosses and wives.

The crack in the depot
waiting for the work orders
to be handed down,
the skiving off to football matches;
the slagging in the canteen,
a mug screwed carefully to the table,
its owner's priceless face when he tried to lift it,
the lads killing themselves laughing.

I wanted in.

Wanted that life.

Never the view from the kitchen.

While the others at school

listened to The Bay City Rollers,
I was knee-deep in Dylan, The Band,
The Allman Brothers Live at Fillmore East.

I'd put in the hours—
long afternoons in the sitting room
on weekends, fire flickering in the grate,
sitting at my brother's feet, leaning
into the speaker to catch the first few notes,
shouting out the name of the artist and song,
bursting with pride when I got it right.

I'd earned my music-lover stripes,
wore my taste like a badge of honour,
so years later, newly-wed and setting up home,
when the man who came to clean the chimney
glanced at the CD rack and said
I see your husband's into music,

I felt stripped of those long afternoons
when I'd first tested the honeyed notes
of a slide guitar on my eager tongue,
foolishly believing the newly-made world
was mine for the taking.

Like when I'd bring the kids

to the doctor and invariably he'd say
Well, what appears to be the problem, Mammy?
and even my smallest, sitting quietly in the pram,
could tell I wasn't this grown man's mammy
so why on earth was he pretending I was?

Or the lovely neighbour

when we brought home our firstborn
who said, upon hearing she was a girl,
You'll have to keep trying for the boy—
spoken in jest, I'm sure,

so why then the tightness in my chest?

One That Got Away

My knight in shining armour, she calls him,
voice still shaky though it's forty years
since her uncle pushed past
their sullen resistance,
stood at the foot of the stairs,
calling up to her to pack her things;
he'd come to bring her home.

Forty years and still she finds it hard
to forgive a mother
cowed by the parish priest
—widowed, without a man
to keep control—
who blackened her ears
with talk of family shame, terrible sin,
righteous solutions to an awful mess
only God knew how to put right.

She's one of the lucky ones,
a narrow escape,
she knows that—
but this tightness
in her throat, hurt rising
when she hears of mothers erased
from birth certificates, of underground tanks,
infant bones pressed up against each other,
endlessly seeking comfort in the dark.

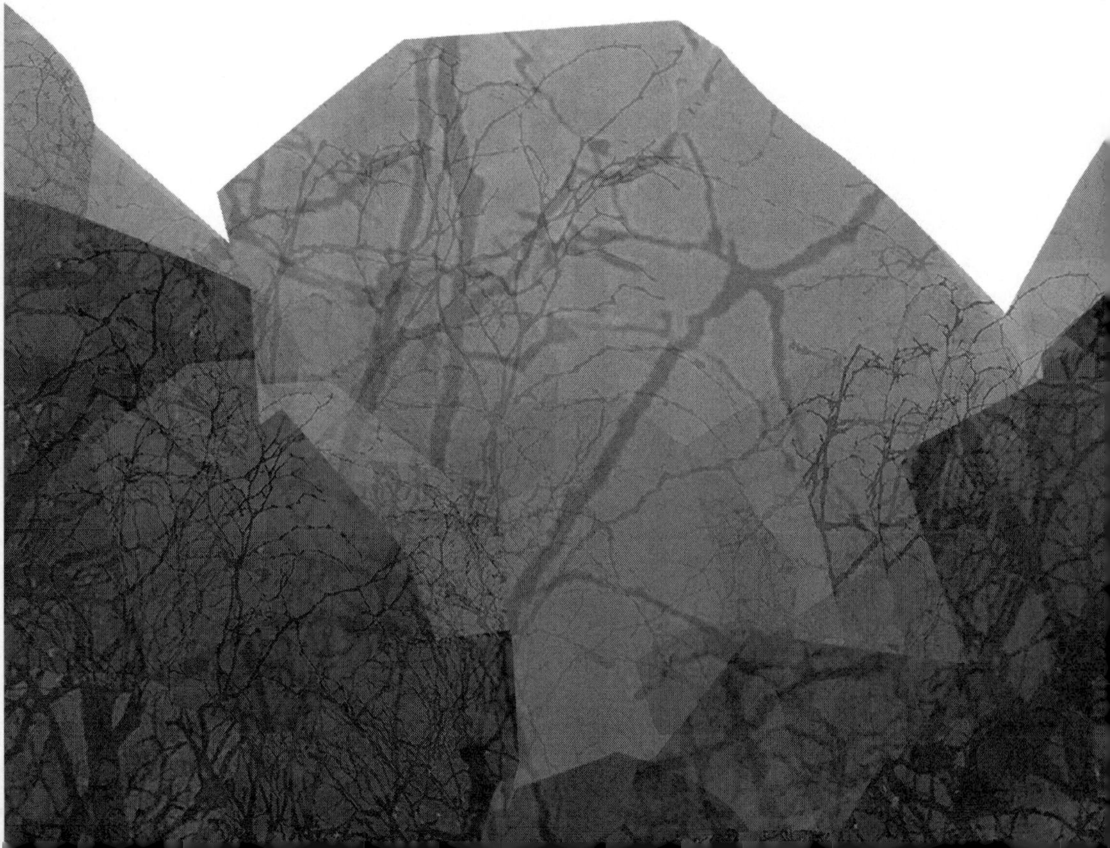

In Conversation (i)

You're sitting opposite me at the kitchen table, apron still on,
like you've just sat down and forgot to take it off.
You look the same as you always did. You look like my mother.

It's been five years and you want to know what's been happening
since, so I tell you Olive died on Christmas Day. Olive dead. Hard
to believe, I know. Your youngest sister.

Maura was in hospital for the funeral. Tom is no longer able to travel
down from Dublin so only Eileen was there to represent the siblings.

You ask about Dad. Dad, who we all thought would go before you,
who sometimes remembers he had a wife, is doing fine.
All the worrying we did. There's a lesson to be learned there.

Have I been down to Cobh since? I was down for the funeral,
but to be honest, since you left, Cobh is a fading photograph
tucked away in a drawer that's hard to open.

Speaking of photographs, that one of you when you were only fifteen,
out by the water's edge, I have stuck to the wall above my desk.
You were just starting out then, younger than my four now,
but you still look like my mother.

You always look like my mother sitting opposite me at the table
and before the light fades you ask *How's Mary* and I'm ashamed
to tell you I haven't rung her in months, but I promise faithfully
to ring this weekend.

I'll admit to

misreading the gold buttons
on the consultant's blazer,
the casually expensive brogues,
his polished vowels,
the eight syllables in his title
emblazoned across the name tag on his chest.

I'll admit to

looking down at Dad, seeing an old, old man
wrapped in a blanket, slippers on his feet;
noting a missing eye, a missing ear,
an army of scabs, red from picking,
marching across his shiny head.

I'll admit to

bristling at how quickly the consultant dismissed me,
manoeuvring the wheelchair behind the curtain,
placing Dad beyond the comfort of my touch,
far from my reassurance that
the doctor will only be checking your heart.

I'll admit to

being taken aback when from behind the curtain
I heard the consultant speak to Dad, man to upright man,
masters of their own proud destinies,
watched them re-emerge; Dad, straighter now,
head held high, chariot steady beneath him.

Into the garden

we went
found a place to sit
under a tree
facing the February sun

sat there together
faces upturned
soaking up the heat

a breeze came
lifted away
the word *dementia*

placing instead
in our mouths
the scented vowels
of a lavender bush
the yellow song
of a late season daffodil

On his 97th Birthday

Across the nursing home an army of carers
go about their daily business of rousing the dead.

He's still asleep, covers pulled back
to reveal the long pyjamaed length of him,
eyes resolutely closed to the world
refusing to let the day begin.

On the wall over his bed, evidence
of his former upright life reprimands him
for sleeping in.

He's past caring,
having long earned the right
to refuse the call of duty.
Taking orders from no one now
he obeys only the regiment of the body:
the rise and fall of his breath,
arms at ease by his side.

Still, the day that's in it,
certain protocols must be followed:
card and gift are placed on the bedside locker,
birthday greetings are spoken in a loud and cheerful voice,
not one but two renditions of the birthday song are sung,
kisses are administered.

His only response—
the opening of one beady eye to calmly
take me in, then back to the serious business at hand:
sleeping the sleep of the innocent,
dreaming the dreams that legends dream.

Resting my head on his chest

to listen to his slow beating heart speak
of what is still sacred between us;
under tissue-thin skin his pacemaker
pushes against my ear,
a door firmly closing, no sound
but the sound of footsteps
ever more distant, ever less familiar.

He speaks only in tongues

to us now, finding new ways
each day to tell us he's leaving.

I'd secretly wished for this,
that it might be his last winter,
but when the nurse calls to say
the snow is falling faster now,
gathering in folds across his bed,
I ask if she could conjure up
a few more days of summer,

afraid there'll be no time
to build a shelter from the cold,
terrified of what might get lost
in the cracks between this season
and the next.

In Conversation (ii)

Someone today asked if I still miss you—
I could not give a simple answer.
It's true, as the years pass, I miss you less,
I hope it doesn't hurt to hear that.
It's also true I miss you more. I miss being your daughter.
I miss all the squandered opportunities to get to know you better.

Yet now you are one of the few constants in my life;
your death remains fixed to a particular point and time,
a solid, immutable fact.

Watching Dad slip away, his mind dissipating, body diminishing,
a reminder to us of how exhausting it was to witness your illness
slowly seeping inwards: the uncertainty, the stops and starts,
the relentless inching towards that singular moment.

And since we spoke last, Tom died, and within the space of a week,
another death left the family reeling. The first death triggering
the second, two immovable facts forever linked, a constant reminder
of how close to death a life can be lived.

Do I still miss you?

Constantly.

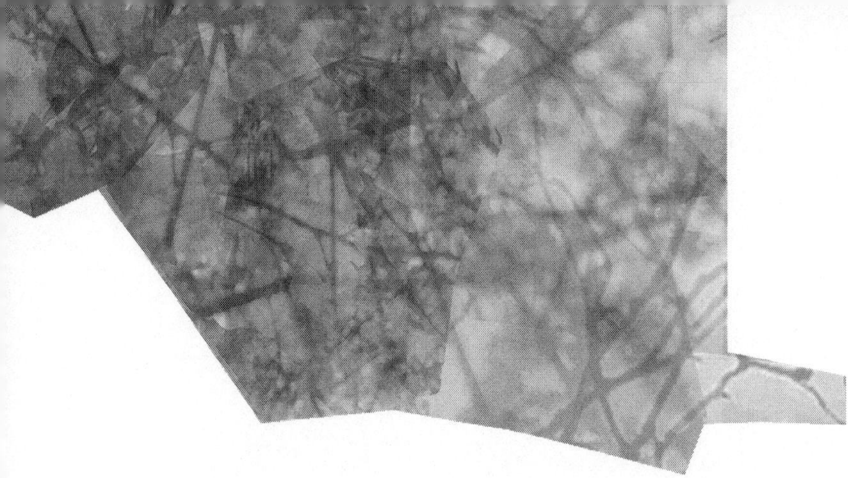

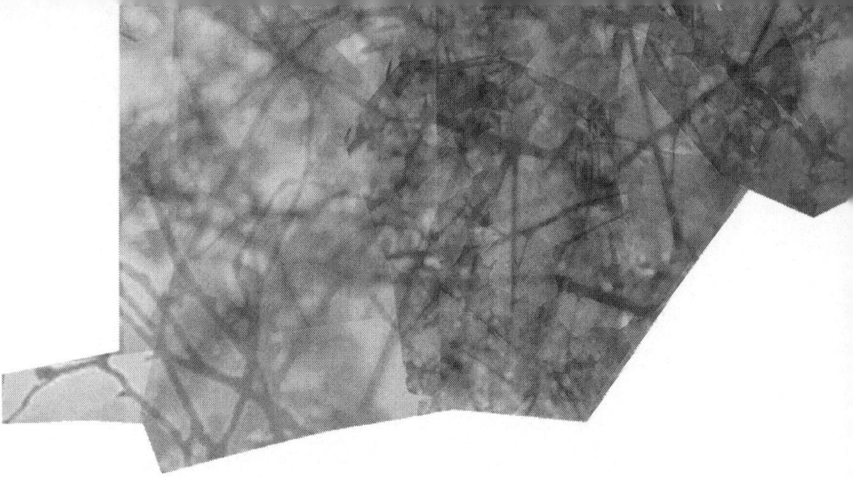

Interview with the Hag

She's standing by the tree on the curve of the river, the one hollowed out by lightning, leaning over the water. When the kids were small, they loved to hide in its blackened hollow, feel the thrill of being close to the river but still safely on land. I'm walking slowly towards her, some distance away but can make her out. Gnarled and scrawny, brown limbs motionless, soot black eyes taking everything in. I've sensed her before and caught sideways glimpses of her outline, but now she's revealed to me, though only from a distance. Taking a step closer, I'm the one being observed; can feel her measuring blood flow, pelvis tilt, heat rising and falling, tissue memory. If I move closer, she'll fade, merge with the wood until I'll wonder if I imagined her. I wait, eyes closed, stand as still as I can, feel the earth steady under me, hear the river beside me, feel the wind move over me. Open my eyes and she's gone. I continue walking past the point of the river where the tree stood many years ago before a storm caught it by the roots, sent it crashing into the water, its charred hollow submerged, unprotected roots exposed.

The Image of

Under the glare of bathroom lights, lines
of invisible ink appear across my face
whispering to me of my mother.
Visual echoes hard to accept,
rivulets of onward-marching age,
crow's feet, a harbinger of what's to come.

I try to look at it from a different angle, come
to my own conclusions, read between the lines;
accede begrudgingly to the outcome of age,
chide the ego, suggest she needs to face-
up to a reality that's hard to accept;
I'm slowly becoming my mother.

How strange that first time my mother
stared at me through my passport photo, come
back to tell me what I struggle to accept;
that time, given time, eventually blurs the lines
between each generation, brings us face to face
with a truth we wrestle with, for an age,

until reluctant wisdom which comes with age
forces us to acquiesce, just like our mothers
before us, to the truth that stares us in the face;
a truth that for each generation comes
when we read in braille, the first fine lines
across our forehead, demanding we accept

the laws that govern every living thing; accept
the passing of time, the shift from youth to age;
accept the laws of the changing seasons, lines
traced in vibrant colour across our mother
earth; accept what's gone and what's to come;
embrace what's etched on the full moon's face.

The mirror in the bathroom, the solemn face
that contemplates my own, asks me to accept
the days, the years ahead, whatever's yet to come;
to inhabit with grace and dignity the age
I am, each season a turn closer to my mother,
mapping her journey, following her lines.

Come, it's good to see again your face,
the lines we share I willingly accept.
Age brings me closer to you, Mother.

Schrödinger's Cat and the Health Scare

(i)

It's a quiet cat—
a ball of silent fur
inside a box
inside her breast.

Four inches long
four inches wide
curled up beneath
one tingling nipple

it's waiting, like her,
for the box to open—
to see if it's dead
or if it's alive.

(ii)

She brings it jogging
along the canal bank walk,
passes the steel bridge
and the trees,
spies swans clustered
beside a stretch of reeds,
observes a dog and his
well-wrapped owner
crossing over at
Blackhorse Bridge;
on the other side
a heron stands off
to the left, staring at the water.
To each she mouths
news of the cat's arrival.

(iii)

One, two weeks pass—
her monthly cycle
bringing changes
to the size and tenderness
of each breast.
The cat shifts, pushes
against the skin,
demanding attention.

(iv)

With a blue felt pen
a dotted circle is drawn
across her skin—
X marks the box.

(v)

Steel
plates
clamp
down
compressing
breast, box, cat—
the blunt shock
erasing all
memory of milk.

(vi)

Eyes on the screen—
ultrasound reveals
a sac of water,
large enough
to drown a cat.

Needle inserted,
liquid drawn out,
box collapses,
long held
breath
                released.

Trade-off

Awake half the night,
hot flushes, the steep hormonal
rise and fall I could well do without,

but it's small price to pay for this bounty—
the universe leaning across the table,
gesturing with both hands,
eager to fill me in.

Glimmer

After Ada Limón

The Japanese have a word for it—*komorebi,*
the play of sunlight filtering through leaves.
This morning the tree outside our house
is almost too beautiful to look at; the turning leaves,
red berries, flickering patterns of light.
On my run, the leggings' waistband presses
against my soft belly, reminding me to keep
a steady pace. Everywhere autumn is shimmering;
trees in Brickfield Park jog slowly past, crunch
and slick of leaves underfoot, slant of light
between the houses. Along the canal
from Golden Bridge to Blackhorse, all life
contained in secret code: seven swans preening
beside a clump of reeds; a heron rising,
wingspan measuring distance from bank to bank;
a moorhen, its red, yellow-tipped beak,
lime green spindle legs, its sheer moor hen-ness.
And everywhere, evidence of our careless nature:
dogshit, cans, plastic wrappers; a wheel,
half covered, glints from under the bridge.
It's my birthday today, and I'm on the lookout
for some sign that all this multiplicity is mapping
a story that's more than the sum of its moving parts.
I pass the cemetery, feet following a small path
under a line of trees. I breathe them in,
they breathe me in. Hidden by their leaves,
along the length of the wall are graffiti runes
and the single word *Soar*—
is this the sign I've been looking for?
Or is it closer to the waters' rippling edge;
a breathless, aging woman,
by a canal, indestructible?

On your birthday

she gave you
a telescope

handed you
the sky

blue rushed in
to fill your lungs

stars rang
in your ears

moons thundered
through your veins

beyond your rim
the heady scent

of a blossoming
universe

bringing galaxies
to their knees

The world is full of trees and hidden creatures

Two hundred and sixty-four million years will pass
before the pulse of a human heart.

Tree trunks rise to more than thirty metres,
sheer, virtually unbranched up to their crowns.

As far as the eye can see—
if there were human eyes to see—
are tangled shades of green and brown;
no flash of colour catches the light
across Carboniferous forest floors.

Silent because nothing knows how to make a noise.

No eardrum captures the vibrations
as a tree topples, crashes to earth;
nor registers the brush of dragon-fly wings,
or the slither of reptiles entering swampy water.

The world is full of trees and hidden creatures.

Mother earth sleeps quietly in the blue-black night,
no restless dreams of what is yet to come.

Darwinius masillae

i

The scientist named her *Ida* after his six-year old daughter, and she,
unfazed by the age gap said, *There are two Idas now:*
there's me, I'm living, and then there's the dead one.

Ida, the dead one, is fossilised perfection.
Ninety-five percent complete, fifty-eight centimetres long
from head to slender tail, she is both here and there:

a whispered outline of skin and fur,
a delicate bridge of tissue and bone
spanning two worlds,
forty-seven million years apart.

ii

Trace back along the curve of time,
decades, centuries, millennia-
still we cannot catch
a glimpse of her beginnings.

iii

Dig
down
deep,
past eras,
epochs, ages,
until we reach the Eocene.

iv

A tiny mammal, lemur-like,
suckling at its mother's breast.

v

At nine months, not yet fully grown,
she forages for food alone. A broken wrist, partially healed,
impedes her climbing but Ida is resourceful, spies beside the lake
some trees, low lying branches yielding fruit and leaves.
Her lips redden, her belly fills.

vi

The lake bubbles up, hot and sulphurous;
noxious fumes fill Ida's lungs.
Losing consciousness she stumbles,
falling headlong into molten silence

the slow, steady descent
lightly crushing
her bones, her skull
settling like silt
in the heavy
darkness.

vii

Swaddled tightly between layers of shale
Ida lies waiting
for slab and partial counter slab to yield,

for eyes to trace the lines of her body,
for a voice to call her by her name.

Separated at Birth

Just 6 million years ago, a single female ape had two daughters.
One became the ancestor of all chimpanzees, the other is our own grandmother.

Some questions perhaps worth considering:

A deliberate act of self-sabotage?

The first instance of sibling rivalry?

Does the mother disown her child?

Does the child disown her mother?

Do the two branches simply grow apart?

Where is the family gathering?

Who gets to trace the family tree?

Boundless

O, reason not the need. Our basest beggars
Are in the poorest thing superfluous.

King Lear

They discovered me buried between two humans;
the place where we lay guarded by basalt blocks
—sprayed red with hematite—
to keep out scavengers, hungry to strip
our carbon-dated bones white clean.

O, the speculation when we were discovered—
perplexed faces hovering above us,
scientific minds grappling with what they'd found.

Was I the first of my kind: *Canis Lupis Familaris,*
my wild lupine ancestors roaming the earth
a thousand score years before?

What purpose did I serve those that lay beside me—
I, who died so young of canine distemper,
unable to hunt, to scavenge; what good was I
to him, to her, to them?

O, foolish questions, foolish minds.

Have you never sat close to a fire, watched sparks rise
into the blue-black, star-blessed sky; the rustling forest
briefly silenced; your hand stroking the soft belly
of the sleeping animal by your side?

An Act of

In 1515, Albrecht Dürer, a German painter and printmaker
produced his now famous woodcutting, *Rhinoceros*.
Like most Europeans, Durer had never seen a rhinoceros,
basing his brilliant if inaccurate impression on written descriptions
and a second-hand sketch.

Rhinoceros (original French title Rhinocéros),
a play written by Eugene Ionesco in 1959,
belongs to the school of drama known as the *Theatre of the Absurd*.
It explores the belief that human existence has no meaning or purpose.

Some Useful Definitions:

extant: still existing, surviving
extinct: family, class or species that has died out
extinction: the act of making extinct; total destruction
and annihilation
phantom limb: the sensation that an amputated or missing limb
is still attached to the body.

Comes Knocking

In the beginning
the signs are easy to miss—
a fish carcass rotting behind the garden shed,
tidemarks on the skirting board,
her boots in the back of the wardrobe,
mildewed and briny.

On Monday the dog goes missing.

Tuesday, every tree in the garden dies;
in the greenhouse, water rises steadily,
crabs hide behind cabbages,
small fish dart between
tomato plants and French beans.

On Wednesday the fridge empties itself.

Thursday, she dreams herself
into the body of a sea lion,
night passing in a silent blue blur
of endless hunting;
the metallic taste of blood
in her mouth when she rises, ravenous,
teeth aching, jaw stiff.

On Friday the power shuts down.

Saturday, she wakes
to roaring in her ears,
the weight of a million
square feet of ice crashing
into the swollen, rising sea.

On Sunday darkness spreads over the deep.

The Poet Transformed into Anger

After Vahni Capildeo

There I was, hollowed out, reckless,
demanding appeasement;
burrowing into the flesh of peaches,
scorching furrows into stone,
teeth gritted, always restless, always
looking for the weakest spot
to chisel, chisel, plunge
into blood-flecked indentations;
grinding, growling, grinning,
reaching for the howl, the harrowing
sensation of crunch, crack,
severed in two. O
love, now there is nothing left
but ache, ache, location unknown.

Event Horizon

Once the dead step
        beyond the rim
the loss is ours not theirs

        to plead with them to return
when the ecstasy of oblivion
        is rushing through them

is to weigh them down
        with a sadness that would enshroud
the earth in mourning

At eighteen I knew nothing

of death and dying, so when a girl from college
told me three of her brothers had drowned
alongside five others, eight bodies in all
recovered from Doolin Bay,
eight lads not much older than I was then,
just down for a weekend music festival,
a scorcher of a day, the sea within shouting distance—
I didn't have the language, didn't know the words,
never thought to ask her brothers' names.

The dead are impatient with us

for our loss of imagination—
we who are
always leaving,

who daily step
blindfolded through
our field of vision,

we who swallow oceans,
we the unchartered

who roll a grain of sand
between finger
and thumb,
fashioning futures
in our own glass image,

we who understand
the sacred
mysteries of loss.

So why now, say the dead,
why now this weeping,
this wringing of hands?

How little the dead remember

it's imagination that terrifies us most,
for in that theatre, loss plays
to an audience of one
over and over and over again—

a little boy wakens from a troubled sleep,
sees his dead mother at the sink, calls out to her;
and when this *almost* mother
turns around to face him,
her cheek is freshly bruised,
her upturned wrists newly slit.

The dead forget it's not the final scene
that paralyses us; it's the nightly return
to our seats, the mind rewinding,
the curtain rising.

My dead mother agrees with me

recalls leaving home at seventeen to work in Dublin;
        her father in uniform standing on the platform,

hands clasped behind his back, growing smaller
        as Kent station curved out of view; the dead weight

of the brown suitcase, the noise of a carriage
        full of strangers, her back pressed up against the unfamiliar

everything; and two years later, the supervisor calling her into his office,
        his voice low, the phone placed against her ear;

the blur of packing, the blur of Heuston station, the terrible motion
        of the train; and the sight of her father, hunched on the platform,

his voice saying her name, handing her the black armband,
        steeling her for what lay still and eternal in her sister's bed.

Orpheus, heartbroken

descends into the underworld
to bring his beloved Eurydice back.

Mothers lean over cots
where changelings lie,
their soft-breathing babies
sleeping beneath fairy hills.

Dreams where fathers,
back from their own funeral,
ring the front door bell
while the living stand in the hall,
caught between hope
and the knowledge
that come morning
they'll have to re-open wounds,
scatter earth again.

I remember thinking
in the days before you died
I might ask you to stay
a while longer,
but when the time came
such a request proved impossible—

with you, pulling away,
and me, watching you leave.

In Conversation (iii)

You're sitting in the front room, reading the paper,
Sally no.3 curled up on the couch beside you.
You look like I remember you before the nursing home days;
you look just like my father.

How did I go in the end? you ask, and I tell you that ever practical,
you gave us one or two weeks soft warning before getting down
to the serious business of slipping away fast. Not dilly-dallying
like the woman in the room beside you who took days to make her peace.

I missed your final breath, sitting outside in the lounge, catching my own,
but you were in good company with Donie holding your hand, singing you
softly out—*sittin' on the dock of the bay, watchin' the tide roll away.*

Then all of us standing round your bed, when one of the residents
came into the room, took a step towards you, tripped on the mat
and fell across your body. We couldn't but laugh.

The women were always falling for me, you remind me,
giving your customary wink. It's true. You were charming the women
right up to the end. One ear, one eye, down to skin and bone
and still flashes of wit, still flashes of the old Des.

Did everyone get enough to eat and drink at the funeral? you ask,
and I inform you that everyone was looked after, as if you were hosting it,
and that we sent you off in style, the bog oak coffin made in Italy,
like your favourite leather shoes.

You know you were a really good father, I tell you, getting ready to leave.
I'm starting to believe it, you say, picking up the paper again, reminding me,
before I go, to pop my head into the kitchen to say hello to Mam,
and not to go missing the wood for the trees.

Turning fifty-two (ii)

Finally, I've got round
to learning the name
of the tree that grows
on the footpath
outside our house—

it's a sycamore.

Alice in Wonderland

CMI Campus, Chennai

There, a tree I've never seen before,
leaves lapping up the midday sun,
and birds, feathered questions, hopping
from branch to hidden branch
before my mouth can find their name.

A lizard circles around the trunk, pauses
so I may admire his poised, intricate
beauty, before his smaller cousin, whippet fast
scurries through a broken canopy of grass,
past toes which curl instinctively.

Picking Figs

She rings me in the early evening
—my first-born lately flown the nest—
to tell me they've been picking figs
from trees growing on his father's land.
She tells me of their plans to *make fig jam.*

I let the phrase settle in my ear,
say it to myself to taste it on my tongue;

close my eyes, see a table set for breakfast
—the Spanish winter sun still warm
across the walls and tiles—
the two of them sitting in easy silence:
one drinking the last of freshly squeezed orange juice,
the other spreading fig jam on crusty bread,

days of such mornings behind them,
days of such mornings ahead.

On our second round

we pass again the tree
covered in pinky-white blossoms

and knowing your way
round a garden
you ask yourself the question
Almond or plum?

While you wait
for the answer
to arrive I revel
in the extravagance
of a universe

that would place so many
blossoms on one tree

and when earth tilts
away from the sun
might offer up
for our pleasure
the exotic scent
of almonds
the purple sweetness
of a plum

Seville

At the bus station
orange trees, unexpected
in an open courtyard;
along the route
to the apartment
orange tree after
orange tree,
fruit ripening
or strewn carelessly
on the path.

Wet streets
seeping through
flimsy footwear
soaking into socks.
Around us, wrapped
in stylish raincoats,
waterproof boots,
umbrellas up or at the ready,
a city revelling in
the novelty of rain.

Labyrinths
of narrow streets,
slick cobblestones,
high castle walls,
street awnings kissing,
cycle lanes moseying,
a bevy of bell-wielding
bikers passing by.

Ensconced
in the apartment
on Calle Jesús de la Vera Cruz,
tiredness scuppering
plans to head out,
two bottles of red
and a couch keep us company,
evening settles in for the night.

We play
I'll see your song
& I'll raise you mine
me on the laptop
you on the phone;
back and forth,
forth and back:
Something in the Way She Moves
The Long & Winding Road
To Sir with Love
Lay Lady Lay—

lay across my big brass bed.

A Bout of Nostalgia

After Billy Collins

Remember that morning in the playground
when all the swings had seats, the slide was dry
and no one had set fire to the swinging tyre?

Remember that lunchtime in Stephen's Green
when it didn't rain, sandwiches weren't soggy,
ducks were in great form, the trees smiling?

Remember that afternoon in Dunnes Stores
when we didn't run over a child's foot with the trolley,
eggs didn't smash, milk didn't spill?

Remember that Saturday evening
when children played happily together,
no cuts or bruises, no teeth marks on the crayons?

Remember that night in the bedroom,
both of us awake at the same time,
the house empty, our eyes glinting in the dark?

A Friday night in January

when you head out, expecting nothing
from the evening; cycle to a charity gig
you'd reluctantly promised to go to

and finding a place to lock the bike
on the square outside
you walk down basement stairs,
the muffled thrum of music, urgent and pulsing,
pushing you through doors into
a teeming crowd swaying in their seats,
buzzing around the bar, sparking off the energy
coming from the low stage

where five members of a middle-aged band
are playing like it's *The Last Waltz*;
like it's their last dance before
the clock strikes twelve

and before you know it
you've stepped off the edge,
stepped into the mystery
of what it means to be in Dublin
in a basement bar, on a Friday night in January

and much, much later, when you re-emerge,
a soft rain is falling on the square, on the trees,
on your bike, on the swans resting on the canal bank,
and on the final stretch of hushed road
an unexpected encore:
a fox appears on the footpath ahead,
crosses the road in front of you,
—the music of her movements a song
in the back of your throat—
before disappearing
through a garden gate
to silent, rapturous applause.

Cycling in Chennai

Srilata lends me her bicycle,
its faded purple frame, rusty gears,
threadbare tyres begging me to love it,
begging me to sit astride its bum-sore saddle
and take to the highways of the college campus;

follow the road flanked with trees, trees
sun-drenched trees, and deer, deer
searching for food in overflowing bins,
birds riding the waves of their dappled backs;

follow, follow, follow the curve, faster
faster into the breeze, past students
cycling in twos and threes,
and as we pass each other by
give them the secret nod that says

hail universal tribe of pedal pushers,
hail kings and queens of forward motion,
hail the triumph of our journey.

Turning fifty-two (iii)

Last year someone gave
me the gift of a hazel tree cutting
which I carried home
on the back of my bike,
before throwing it
in the corner of the garage
where it lay un-watered for six months
before the man of the house
took it upon himself to dig a random hole
in the front garden and plant it there.

When I turned fifty-two last October
I saw the knee-high hazel tree
planted there in our front garden,
and took to watering it every week,
took to chatting with it,
took to admiring
its tightly held secrets
until one morning
in spring, I opened my eyes
and there, where once
was only brown,
twenty-six letters of
a new alphabet
unfurled in green—
the answer to a question
I'd been too afraid to ask.

In Loving Memory of Thomas Desmond (Des) Tannam

31st January 1922 – 20th November 2019

Afterthought

A mother speaks

of her daughter's birth:
the deafening absence
of a heartbeat,
the stillness of the body,
the time of death announced

and how she asked to hold
her daughter, removed the blanket,
placed the perfect body against her own,
called out to her partner to lie beside them,
offer his warmth to their daughter;
and together they placed incantations
into the whorls of her exquisite ears:
the story of her welcome,
her given name,
the excitement of her siblings,
the buttery warmth of the yellow
they'd chosen for the nursery walls,
her place in the scheme of their lives

and as they weaved the story round her
a filigree of breath, beyond the realms
of science and medicine, flared
in each of her nostrils, filled her lungs;
the rise and fall of her chest
pressing up against their words,
demanding to hear more.

References

DEDICATION PAGE

The quote *my suspect edifice upright in air, as Atlas did the sky* is from the poem 'Atlas' by UA Fanthorpe (Safe as House, Peterloo Poets 1995)

HOME SWEET HOME

Little pig, little pig, let me in etc. is an excerpt from the folktale and fable *The Three Little Pigs*

And I am praying to God most high etc.is an excerpt from Padraic Colum's poem *An Old Woman of the Roads* (Selected Poems of Padraic Colum, Syracuse Press 1989)

The world is full of trees

All lines in italics are from *Life A Natural History Of The First Four Billion Years Of Life On Earth*, Richard Fortey (Vintage Books).

DARWINIUS MASILLAE

Darwinius masillae (nickname Ida) represents the most complete fossil primate ever found, including both skeleton, soft body outline and contents of the digestive tract. She was discovered in 1983 in a disused quarry pit near Messel village in Germany.

SEPARATED AT BIRTH

The quote Just 6 million years ago, a single female ape had two daughters. One became the ancestor of all chimpanzees, the other is our own grandmother comes from Yuval Noah Harari's *Sapiens A Brief History of Humankind* (Vintage Books 2015)

AT EIGHTEEN I KNEW NOTHING

This poem recalls the tragic drowning on the 31st July, 1983 of eight young people attending the Lisdoonvarna Festival. Among the eight dead were three brothers: James, John and Eddie Doran.

SEVILLE

The following songs are quoted in this poem: *Something* by the Beatles (Abbey Road 1969), *The Long and Winding Road* by the Beatles (Let It Be 1970), *To Sir With Love*, sung by Lulu (Lyric: Don Black / Music: Mark London) and *Lay Lady Lay* by Bob Dylan (Nashville Skyline 1969)

ANNE TANNAM is the author of two poetry collection, *Take This Life* (Wordonthestreet 2011) and *Tides Shifting Across My Sitting Room Floor* (Salmon Poetry 2017). The winner of the 40 Word Competition, 2019 (Bangor Literary Journal) and Poetry Day Ireland Competition 2018 (Books Upstairs), her work was highly commended in the Francis Ledwidge Awards and shortlisted in the Baileoborough Awards. Her work has been published widely in literary journals and on national radio and print. Anne was poet-in-residence at the Trim Poetry Festival in 2020 and was awarded a writers' residency at Chennai Mathematical Institute in Chennai, India in 2016.

A spoken word poet, Anne has been invited to perform her work at various festivals and events at home and abroad including Electric Picnic, Lingo, Bloom, The Kosovo International Poetry Festival, The Craw Festival (Berlin), Lumen Poetry Series (London) and The Bray Literary Festival. For more information on Anne's poetry, visit her website www.annetannampoetry.ie.

salmonpoetry

Cliffs of Moher, County Clare, Ireland

"Like the sea-run Steelhead salmon that thrashes upstream to its spawning ground, then instead of dying, returns to the sea—Salmon Poetry Press brings precious cargo to both Ireland and America in the poetry it publishes, then carries that select work to its readership against incalculable odds."

TESS GALLAGHER

The Salmon Bookshop & Literary Centre

Ennistymon, County Clare, Ireland

"Another wonderful Clare outlet."
The Irish Times, 35 Best Independent Bookshops